LITERATURE AND CRITICAL THINKING

Art Projects • Bulletin Boards • Summaries
Skill Building Activities • Independent Thinking

Written by: John and Patty Carratello

Illustrated by: Anna Chellton, Paula Spence, Keith Vasconcelles, and Theresa Wright

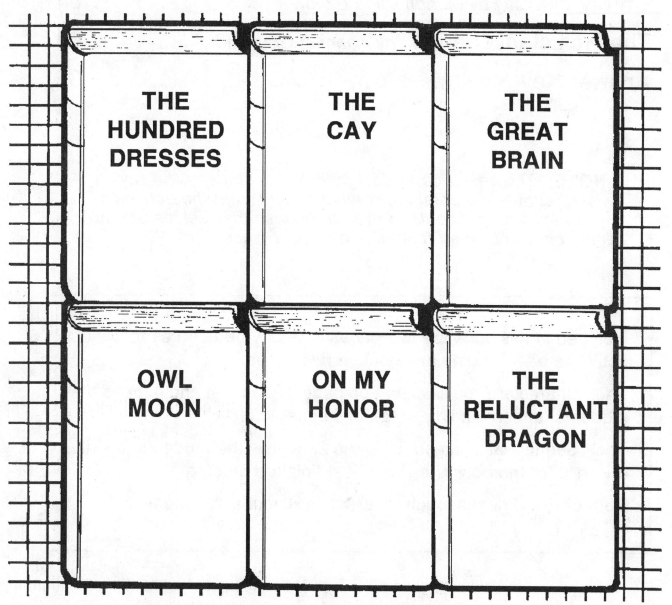

THE HUNDRED DRESSES

THE CAY

THE GREAT BRAIN

OWL MOON

ON MY HONOR

THE RELUCTANT DRAGON

Teacher Created Materials, Inc.
P. O. Box 1214
Huntington Beach, CA 92649
© Teacher Created Materials, Inc. 1989
Made in U. S. A.

TABLE OF CONTENTS

NOTE: *This resource is designed to accompany the books listed above. To obtain maximum benefit from the activities, you may want students to read the books themselves or you may choose to read them aloud to your class.*

Included in this book are two pages that may be used as follow-up activities after reading any book in this series.

The "Character Profile Sheet" on page 21 can test and expand the students' understanding of the main character(s).

The "Sequel" assignment on page 22 allows the students to write a Part II for the book they have just finished reading.

Both of these pages touch all areas in Bloom's Taxonomy.

INTRODUCTION

LITERATURE AND CRITICAL THINKING

It is possible for all children at varying developmental levels to engage in a discovery process which clarifies thinking, increases knowledge, and deepens their understanding of human issues and social values. This activities book, based on Bloom's *Taxonomy of Skills in the Cognitive Domain*, provides teachers a resource to maximize this process, using distinguished children's literature as a vehicle.

The authors suggest the following options in using this book:

OPTION 1: The teacher may select a single activity for the entire class.

OPTION 2: The teacher may select different activities for single students or small groups of students.

OPTION 3: The student may select the level at which he or she wishes to work, once the teacher explains what is available.

The stories in this book follow the same format, so that each level of thinking skills is approached as follows:

KNOWLEDGE

This level provides the child with an opportunity to recall fundamental facts and information about the story. Success at this level will be evidenced by the child's ability to:

- Match character names with pictures of the characters.
- Identify the main characters in a crossword puzzle.
- Match statements with the characters who said them.
- List the main characteristics of one of the main characters in a WANTED poster.
- Arrange scrambled story pictures in sequential order.
- Arrange scrambled story sentences in sequential order.
- Recall details about the setting by creating a picture of where a part of the story took place.

COMPREHENSION

This level provides the child with an opportunity to demonstrate a basic understanding of the story. Success at this level will be evidenced by the child's ability to:

- Interpret pictures of scenes from the story.
- Explain selected ideas or parts from the story in his or her own words.

COMPREHENSION

- Draw a picture showing what happened before and after a passage or illustration found in the book.
- Write a sentence explaining what happened before and after a passage or illustration found in the book.
- Predict what could happen next in the story before the reading of the entire book is completed.
- Construct a pictorial time line which summarizes what happens in the story.
- Explain how the main character felt at the beginning, middle, and/or end of the story.

APPLICATION

This level provides the child with an opportunity to use information from the story in a new way. Success at this level will be evidenced by the child's ability to:

- Classify the characters as human, animal, or thing.
- Transfer a main character to a new setting.
- Make finger puppets and act out a part of the story.
- Select a meal that one of the main characters would enjoy eating, plan a menu, and a method of serving it.
- Think of a situation that occurred to a character in the story and write about how he or she would have handled the situation differently.
- Give examples of people the child knows who have the same problems as the characters in the story.

ANALYSIS

This level provides the child with an opportunity to take parts of the story and examine these parts carefully in order to better understand the whole story. Success at this level will be evidenced by the child's ability to:

- Identify general characteristics (stated and/or implied) of the main characters.
- Distinguish what could happen from what couldn't happen in the story in real life.
- Select parts of the story that were funniest, saddest, happiest, and most unbelievable.
- Differentiate fact from opinion.
- Compare and/or contrast two of the main characters.
- Select an action of a main character that was exactly the same as something the child would have done.

SYNTHESIS

This level provides the child with an opportunity to put parts from the story together in a new way to form a new idea or product. Success at this level will be evidenced by the child's ability to:

- Create a story from just the title before the story is read (pre-story exercise).
- Write three new titles for the story that would give a good idea what it was about.
- Create a poster to advertise the story so people will want to read it.
- Create a new product related to the story.
- Restructure the roles of the main characters to create new outcomes in the story.
- Compose and perform a dialogue or monologue that will communicate the thoughts of the main character(s) at a given point in the story.
- Imagine that he or she is one of the main characters and write a diary account of daily thoughts and activities.
- Create an original character and tell how the character would fit into the story.
- Write the lyrics and music to a song that one of the main characters would sing if he/she/it became a rock star - and perform it.

EVALUATION

This level provides the child with an opportunity to form and present an opinion backed up by sound reasoning. Success at this level will be evidenced by the child's ability to:

- Decide which character in the selection he or she would most like to spend a day with and why.
- Judge whether or not a character should have acted in a particular way and why.
- Decide if the story really could have happened and justify reasons for the decision.
- Consider how this story can help the child in his or her own life.
- Appraise the value of the story.
- Compare the story with another one the child has read.
- Write a recommendation as to why the books should be read or not.

In addition to the activities just outlined, a class project and a small group project will be included for each story.

The Hundred Dresses

by Eleanor Estes

Wanda Petronski has missed several days of school. This greatly disheartens some of the girls in Room 13, for now they have no one to tease. Teasing is easy when the girl who says she has "one hundred dresses" wears the same faded and worn blue dress daily to school.

But Wanda **does** have one hundred dresses — the beautiful drawings of the dresses her imagination owns. Her pictures are so lovely that her artwork wins the medal for the fashion design contest and the admiration of her peers. However, the students in Room 13 learn that Mr. Petronski has moved away to the city because of the prejudicial behavior that had been cruelly directed toward his children.

One girl, so deeply moved by the unhappiness she helped to cause for the Petronski family, learns a painful lesson about caring and equality. And she does what she can to make this wrong right.

The House on Boggins Heights

Peggy and Maddie went to Wanda's house on Boggins Heights after school. Describe what they saw when they opened the door and looked inside her house.

KNOWLEDGE: Activity 2

Who?

Match the quotes with the characters who said or thought them.

> **Jan Petronski**   **Maddie**
>
> **Peggy**   **Jake**
>
> **Miss Mason**   **Wanda**

1. "I am sure none of my boys and girls in Room 13 would purposely and deliberately hurt anyone's feelings because his name happened to be a long unfamiliar one."

2. "I have done just as much as Peggy to make life miserable for Wanda by simply standing by and saying nothing."

3. "I'd like that girl Peggy to have the drawing of the green dress with the red trimming and her friend Maddie to have the blue one. For Christmas."

4. "Wanda, tell us. How many dresses did you say you had hanging up in your closet?"

5. "I wish Peggy would stop teasing Wanda."

6. "I gotta hurry. I gotta get the doors open and ring the bell."

7. "I got a hundred dresses home."

8. "Now we move away to big city. No more holler Polack. No more ask why funny name. Plenty of funny names in the big city."

9. "I never did call her a foreigner or make fun of her name. I never thought she had the sense to know we were making fun of her anyway."

10. "Why, it really looks like me! Wanda had really drawn this for me!"

#362 Literature & Critical Thinking, Book 8   8   © Teacher Created Materials, Inc. 1989

The Bulletin Board

Draw what the students in Room 13 found on the bulletin board the day the contest winners were announced.

1. Why were these pictures on the bulletin board?

   _____

   _____

   _____

2. How did the students feel when they saw the pictures?

   _____

   _____

   _____

3. What could the students do about how they felt?

   _____

   _____

Meaning

Explain what these quotes from the story mean.

1. "But suppose Peggy and all the others started in on her next! She wasn't poor as Wanda perhaps, but she was poor. Of course she would have more sense than to say a hundred dresses. Still she would not like them to begin on her. Not at all!" (Chapter 2)

_____

_____

_____

_____

2. "For now Peggy seemed to think a day was lost if she had not had some fun with Wanda, winning the approving laughter of the girls." (Chapter 3)

_____

_____

_____

_____

3. "Dear teacher: My Wanda will not come to your school anymore. Jake also. Now we move away to big city. No more holler Pollack. No more ask why funny name. Plenty of funny names in the big city. Yours truly, Jan Petronski." (Chapter 5)

_____

_____

_____

_____

4. "At last Maddie sat up in bed and pressed her forehead tight in her hands and really thought. This was the hardest thinking she had ever done. After a long, long time she reached an important conclusion. She was never going to stand by and say nothing again." (Chapter 6)

_____

_____

_____

_____

Letter To Wanda

You are in Room 13 and have just heard Mr. Petronski's letter. Miss Mason has asked each member of the class to write a letter to Wanda. What would you write to her?

_____

_____ ,

_____

_____

_____

_____

_____

_____

_____

_____

_____

_____ ,

_____

Wanda's Reply

Wanda has received your letter and is ready to reply. What would she say to you? How would she decorate the letter?

_____

_____ ,

_____

_____

_____

_____

_____

_____

_____

_____

_____

_____ ,

_____

The Gift

Wanda gave Peggy and Maddie two dress designs for Christmas presents. Now the girls want to give a gift to Wanda.

What type of gift do you you think would really make Wanda happy? _____

_____

_____

_____

_____

_____

What type of gift do you think would make Peggy and Maddie happy to give to Wanda? _____

_____

_____

_____

_____

How would Wanda receive her present? _____

_____

_____

_____

_____

_____

_____

_____

_____

The Differences

Write at least **three** ways Peggy and Maddie are **different**.

Peggy

_____

_____

_____

_____

Maddie

_____

_____

_____

_____

Read what you have written above. Which things that you have written describe **you?**

_____

_____

_____

_____

_____

Who Would Do This?

Which one of the characters in the story would be the most likely to do the things on this page?

> ## Wanda   Peggy   Maddie

1. not realize that she is being cruel: _____

2. show kindness to someone who hurts her: _____

3. invent a fantasy world to keep her happy: _____

4. defend a person who is being teased: _____

5. not worry about a person's feelings because the person doesn't cry: _____

6. draw all of her life: _____

7. stand up to a friend and tell that friend she is wrong: _____

8. be so excited to be a part of a group that teasing doesn't matter: _____

9. make fun of someone else to entertain others: _____

10. cry because someone innocent is treated unkindly: _____

Which actions on this page would you be most likely to do? Write the numbers here.

_____ _____ _____ _____ _____

_____ _____ _____ _____ _____

Are you more like Wanda, Peggy, or Maddie? _____

Why? _____

_____

_____

_____

_____

_____

_____

_____

DESIGN SHOW

Design a car. Cut out and display your idea in class. Choose a best car design winner!

DESIGN SHOW

Design clothes for a person, male or female. Cut out and display your idea in class. Choose a best clothes design winner!

City Reunion

Work in groups of three for this project.

Maddie and Peggy decide to visit Wanda in the city during vacation. Write what you think the girls will say and do when they see each other.

Our group members:

_____

_____

The Reunion:

_____

_____

_____

_____

_____

_____

_____

_____

_____

_____

_____

_____

_____

_____

Perform your ideas in front of the class if you want!

Wanda's 100 Dresses

1. Why do you think Wanda told Peggy that she had 100 dresses?

   _____

   _____

   _____

2. Do you think Wanda knew she was being teased by the other girls?

   _____

3. What do you think the 100 dresses game really meant to Wanda?

   _____

   _____

   _____

4. Why do you think Wanda decided to give Peggy and Maddie two dress designs for Christmas presents?

   _____

   _____

   _____

5. What do you think Wanda was like as a person?

   _____

   _____

   _____

And You?

Do you ever tease someone else because he or she is different from you? _____

Explain. _____

_____

_____

_____

If you heard someone else teasing a person because of his or her differences, what would you do? _____

_____

_____

_____

_____

_____

_____

What is worse – doing something wrong (like teasing) or doing nothing when you know something wrong is being done? _____

Explain. _____

_____

_____

_____

_____

_____

_____

_____

CHARACTER PROFILE

Develop one of the main characters in the story into a real person. As you fill in these blanks, try to be in the mind of the characters.

Book _____

Author _____

Name of Character _____

Age _____ Height _____ Weight _____ Male or Female _____

Hair Color _____ Eye Color _____ Skin Color _____

1. Where does he/she live? _____
   _____

2. What kind of job does he/she have or would like to have?
   _____

   Why? _____
   _____
   _____

3. Who is his/her best friend? _____
   _____

4. Does he/she have any enemies? _____
   _____

5. Does he/she like life? _____
   _____

6. Fill in these blanks with his/her favorites.
   Color _____ Food _____
   Animal _____ Hobby _____
   Sport _____ Music _____
   Place to go _____
   Thing to do _____
   _____

7. Would you like to have this character as a friend? _____
   Explain _____
   _____
   _____
   _____
   _____

SEQUEL!

You have been chosen to write a sequel (Part II) for the book you have just finished reading. Fill in the blanks below. Then write an explanation of what will happen in your new book!

Title of the book you read: _____

_____

Author: _____

Title of the new book you will write: _____

_____

Your name: _____

Setting (time and location) of the new book: _____

_____

_____

Is this the same setting as in Part I? _____ Explain: _____

Protagonist (main character) of the new book: _____

_____

Description of protagonist: _____

_____

Is this the same protagonist as in Part I? _____ Explain:_____

_____

Antagonist (person or thing causing protagonist conflict) of the new book: _____

_____

Description of antagonist: _____

_____

_____

Is this the same antagonist as in Part I? _____ Explain: _____

_____

What are some things that are the same in each book? _____

_____

_____

_____

What are some things that are different in each book? _____

_____

_____

_____

On the back of this page or on another sheet of paper, write an explanation of what will happen in your new book. Share your ideas with your class!

The Cay
by Theodore Taylor

It is in a time of war, and the war has come to the Caribbean. Phillip and his mother decide to leave for the safety of Virginia, with Phillip's father remaining on the island of Curacao to continue his work for the war effort.

Their escape boat, however, is torpedoed, causing Phillip to suffer a blow to his head that knocks him overboard and renders him unconscious. When he awakens, he finds himself on a raft, tended to by an old man named Timothy. The raft carries Phillip, Timothy, and a black and grey cat for days upon the sea, during which time Phillip loses his sight.

When Timothy sights a cay, a tiny, coral-reefed island, he navigates toward it. It is on the cay that Timothy and Phillip work together to help Phillip become self-sufficient in his blindness. The two have many differences, but chief in Phillip's mind is their difference in color — Timothy is a black man and Phillip is white. However, as the need to survive pulls them together, the color line between them vanishes and they become friends.

It is this friendship that is the key to their survival and the bond that keeps racial discrimination from being a part of Phillip's life, long after a hurricane claims Timothy and Phillip returns home.

SEQUENCE OF EVENTS

Here is a list of events from the story. Rewrite them in the order they happen.

1. Phillip loses his sight.

2. Henrik and Phillip watch the war preparations on Curacao.

3. Timothy dies on the cay.

4. The boat carrying Phillip toward Virginia is torpedoed.

5. Timothy teaches Phillip to weave mats.

6. Timothy saves Phillip from the sharks by the raft.

7. Phillip is rescued.

8. The hurricane whips over the cay.

9. A moray eel bites Phillip.

10. Phillip returns home to his mother and father.

1. _____

2. _____

3. _____

4. _____

5. _____

6. _____

7. _____

8. _____

9. _____

10. _____

WANTED!

Create a wanted poster for Timothy.

WANTED

Timothy

age: _____

physical description:_____

_____

_____

favorite words:_____

personality description: _____

_____

_____

_____

special friends: _____

The Hurricane

Draw the way Phillip and Timothy protected themselves during the hurricane.

1. What is happening in this picture? _____
    _____

2. What happens after this picture? _____
    _____

3. What does it show about Timothy's knowledge of hurricanes? _____
    _____
    _____

4. How does it show the relationship between Phillip and Timothy? _____
    _____
    _____

The Change

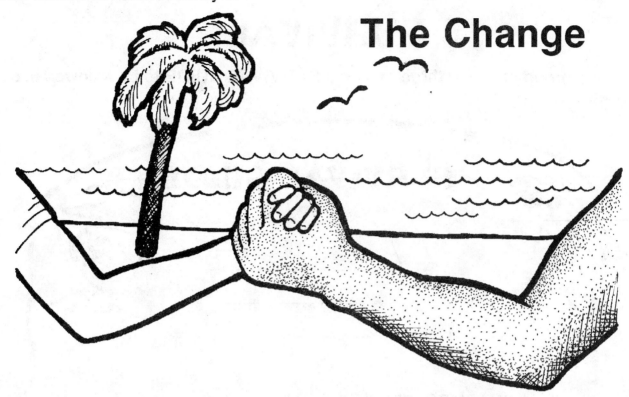

Explain how each of these quotes reflects Phillip's attitude toward Timothy.

1.   "My father had always taught me to address anyone I took to be an adult as 'mister,' but Timothy didn't seem to be a mister. Besides, he was black."

    _____

    _____

    _____

2.   "I said to Timothy, 'I want to be your friend.' He said softly, 'Young bahss, you 'ave always been my friend!' "

    _____

    _____

    _____

3.   "I moved close to Timothy's big body before I went to sleep. I remember smiling in the darkness. He felt neither white nor black."

    _____

    _____

    _____

4.   "I asked, 'Timothy, are you still black?' "

    _____

    _____

    _____

SURVIVAL!

Work in a group of two or three to plan a SURVIVAL GUIDE to be followed in case of disaster.

SURVIVAL GUIDE

by

_____

_____

_____

SUPPLIES WE MUST HAVE: _____

_____

_____

_____

JOBS WE MUST DO: _____

_____

_____

_____

RULES WE MUST FOLLOW: _____

_____

_____

_____

PRECAUTIONS WE MUST TAKE:_____

_____

_____

_____

_____

_____

APPLICATION: Activity 2

Return To The Cay

An older Phillip has just navigated through the Devil's Mouth and found his cay. He goes ashore.

Write a description of what Phillip thinks, does, and says.

_____

_____

_____

_____

_____

_____

_____

_____

_____

_____

_____

_____

_____

_____

_____

_____

_____

_____

_____

_____

_____

You Choose!

1. What part of the story was the most frightening?

_____

_____

_____

2. What part of the story was full of the most action?

_____

_____

_____

3. What part of the story was the saddest?

_____

_____

_____

4. What part of the story was the most believable?

_____

_____

_____

5. What part of the story was the most meaningful to you?

_____

_____

_____

_____

_____

"Dat Be True?"

Read these sentences about things and people in the story. Write TRUE or FALSE next to each question.

1. _____ It is Phillip who wants most to escape to Virginia.

2. _____ After the shipwreck, Phillip is very happy to regain consciousness on a raft with a strong, black, old man.

3. _____ Stew Cat is important to Phillip's comfort.

4. _____ Climbing for coconuts means more to Phillip than just food and milk.

5. _____ Timothy is a selfish man.

6. _____ Phillip is completely useless because of his blindness.

7. _____ Timothy cannot read.

8. _____ Timothy teaches Phillip important lessons.

9. _____ Phillip and Timothy both save each other's lives.

10. _____ After the devastation caused by the hurricane, Phillip does not have the interest or ability to rebuild a "home."

11. _____ Phillip feels that he could survive another hurricane on the cay.

12. _____ Phillip's relationship with Timothy changes his relationship with black people.

OUTRAGEOUS!

Phillip finds that the "soft and beautiful West Indian accent and way of speaking" aren't always clear.

Do you and the rest of your classmates understand Timothy? Here are some sentences to "translate".

1. "We mebbe 'ere two, tree days. So we be libin' comfortable."

   _____

   _____

   _____

   _____

2. "D'mahn in d'sky, of course."

   _____

   _____

   _____

3. "Why b'feesh different color, or flower b'different color? I true don' know, Phill-eep, but I true tink beneath d'skin is all d'same."

   _____

   _____

   _____

   _____

Locate four of Timothy's quotes that you feel will "stump" your classmates. Share the passages with the class. See if anyone can translate them! Can you?

Quote #1, page _____   Quote #2, page _____

Quote #3, page _____   Quote #4, page _____

What If...

What if Timothy had not died on the cay? What if he was rescued along with Phillip? What would their relationship be like?

Work with a partner to create a dialogue between them that begins as they step off the rescue boat together at Curacao. Use the back of this sheet if necessary.

_____   _____
                                           _____
                                           _____
                                           _____
_____   _____
                                           _____
                                           _____
_____   _____
                                           _____
                                           _____
                                           _____
_____   _____
                                           _____
                                           _____
                                           _____
_____   _____
                                           _____
                                           _____
                                           _____
_____   _____
                                           _____
                                           _____
                                           _____
_____   _____
                                           _____

The Cay

1. What did Phillip learn on the cay?

   _____

   _____

   _____

   _____

2. Could he have learned the same things at home or in school? Explain.

   _____

   _____

   _____

3. Why did Timothy give so much of himself to Phillip?

   _____

   _____

   _____

   _____

4. Would Timothy have treated Phillip the same if they had met in town or on a boat dock? _____ Explain.

   _____

   _____

   _____

   _____

5. What did their experience on the cay do for their relationship?

   _____

   _____

   _____

   _____

34

The Dream

Theodore Taylor dedicates his book in this way:

"To Dr. King's dream, which can only come true if the very young know and understand."

Dr. King is Dr. Martin Luther King, Jr. He had a dream that one day everyone would join hands together like sisters and brothers and sing in equality and peace.

1. Knowing this about Dr. King, what do you think Theodore Taylor means by his book dedication?

   _____

   _____

   _____

   _____

   _____

   _____

2. Do Timothy and Phillip "live up" to Dr. King's dream? _____ Explain.

   _____

   _____

   _____

   _____

   _____

3. Do you try to live this way? _____ Explain.

   _____

   _____

   _____

   _____

   _____

The Great Brain

by John D. Fitzgerald

John idolizes his brother Tom. For when a problem of any kind arises, it is Tom who puts his great brain to work and soon the problem is solved.

The Great Brain, as Tom is called, tackles these problems with a style all his own, and grand adventures follow. He plans a rescue for the Jensen boys lost in Skeleton Cave, creates a scandal about the strict, new school teacher, and attempts to make money with nearly every other idea he has. Tom is a classy con artist and there is not a child with a coin or a new toy who is safe from his scheming ways.

But there is another side to the boy with ideas. Despite his conniving ways, Tom has a sense of empathy with people. Abie (out of place and alone because of his religion), Basil (teased because of his immigrant status), and Andy (intent upon suicide because of his crippling accident), all are touched by Tom as he helps them against the odds.

The Great Brain is a story about boyhood pranks and adventures — and a story about compassion and love.

Character Match!

Match these characters with their descriptions.

```
a.  Mr. Standish          f.  Tom

b.  Uncle Mark            g.  Abie

c.  John                  h.  Andy

d.  Howard                i.  Basil

e.  Mamma                 j.  Papa
```

1. _____ has hands that are never idle. They are busy sewing, cooking, washing, and always moving.

2. _____ has difficulty letting any opportunity to make money go by untried.

3. _____ tries to commit suicide because of being "plumb useless."

4. _____ doesn't understand American ways and must fight in order to be accepted.

5. _____ idolizes an older brother.

6. _____ can't resist ordering any new invention.

7. _____ starves to death because of pride.

8. _____ is the town sheriff.

9. _____ infects J.D. with the mumps at J.D.'s request.

10. _____ punishes children unfairly and uses a paddle to do so.

BACKFIRE!

Not all the plans in the story were ones that worked.
Explain how each of these ideas failed.

1. Tom charges the children in town one penny to
   see the new water closet.

   _____

   _____

   _____

   _____

   _____

   _____

2. John catches the mumps first so he can infect his older brothers in order to
   laugh at them and tease them.

   _____

   _____

   _____

   _____

3. Tom and some other school children frame the new, mean school teacher
   so he will be fired.

   _____

   _____

   _____

   _____

   _____

   _____

   _____

   _____

The Turning Point

The action that is happening in this picture shows a turning point in Tom's personality. Explain how Tom has just changed.

_____

_____

_____

_____

_____

_____

_____

_____

_____

Why Was This Said?

Explain why each of these quotes from the story was said.

1. "What men like Mr. Leeds fail to understand is that it is the mingling of different cultures, talents, and know-how of the different nationalities which will one day make this the greatest nation on earth." (Papa to Tom about Sammy Leeds' father — Chapter 5)

_____

_____

_____

_____

_____

2. "It wasn't empty. It contained a man's most priceless possession." (Mama about Abie — Chapter 6)

_____

_____

_____

_____

_____

_____

3. "Please, J.D. if you love me as a brother you will take back the belt. I'm not sick. I give you my word." (Tom to J.D. — Chapter 8)

_____

_____

_____

_____

_____

If You Were Tom...

1. If you were Tom, would you have charged your friends money to watch construction in your yard?

   _____

   Explain._____

   _____

   _____

   _____

   _____

   _____

2. If you were Tom, would you have told someone about Abie's empty strongbox? _____

   Explain._____

   _____

   _____

   _____

   _____

   _____

   _____

   _____

3. If you were Tom, would you have given back the erector set?_____

   Explain._____

   _____

   _____

   _____

   _____

   _____

Here I Am!

Tom has just been transported to your time and is sitting in your classroom.

The first thing Tom would do is

_____

_____

_____

The first thing Tom would say is _____

_____

_____

_____

Would he be accepted? _____ Explain._____

_____

_____

Would he have a fight? _____ Explain._____

_____

_____

Would he like you? _____

_____

Would he like your teacher? _____

_____

What subject would he like most?_____

What subject would he like least?_____

Who would his friends be? _____

_____

_____

42

IDEAS FROM THE GREAT BRAIN!

1. Explain how one of Tom's ideas showed his smart thinking.

   _____

   _____

   _____

   _____

2. Explain how one of Tom's ideas showed his courage.

   _____

   _____

   _____

   _____

3. Explain how one of Tom's ideas showed his caring for other people.

   _____

   _____

   _____

   _____

4. Explain how one of Tom's ideas showed he loved to make money.

   _____

   _____

   _____

   _____

5. Which one of Tom's ideas could you have thought of, too?

   _____

   _____

   _____

   _____

THE TRUTH!

Analyze the truth in these quotes.

1. "To take part in anything that is wrong even one percent is just as bad as one hundred percent." (Mamma — Chapter 1)

   How is this quote true in the story? _____

   _____

   _____

   Is this quote true for you?_____

   Explain. _____

   _____

2. "I knew the only way to make Sammy stop picking on me was to keep on fighting him until I could lick him. Now we are friends." (Tom — Chapter 5)

   How is this quote true in the story? _____

   _____

   _____

   Is this quote true for you?_____

   Explain. _____

   _____

3. "All the kids in town had been forbidden by their parents to play in the barn after Seth's accident. What parents didn't seem to realize was that this was one sure way to make us kids play in the barn." (Chapter 7)

   How is this quote true in the story? _____

   _____

   _____

   Is this quote true for you?_____

   Explain. _____

   _____

44

Inside The Great Brain

This story is told by John. We hear how Tom feels only through what John reports Tom says and does.

Choose one incident from the story. Go inside the mind of The Great Brain. Tell us what Tom **THINKS** as this one incident is happening.

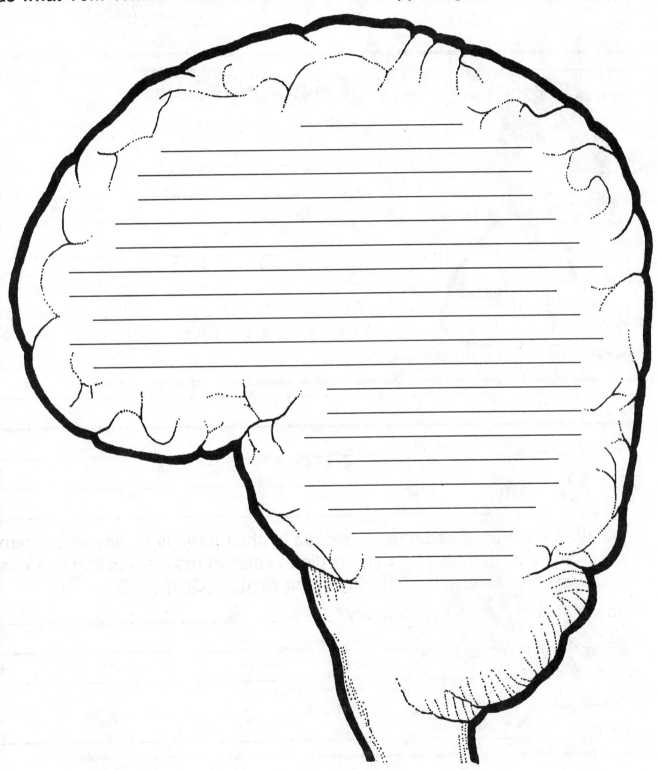

The Problem!

Each class member gets one of these strips. On the strip, he or she writes a problem for The Great Brain to solve. The teacher collects all the strips and puts them in a box. Then, each class member chooses a problem from the box, writes a solution to that problem on the solution strip (found on page 2 of this activity) and reads both strips to the class.

The Solution!

Each class member gets one of these strips. He or she is to use the strip to write the solution for the problem described on page 1 of this activity.

Is It Wrong?

Are these things that happen in the story right or wrong? Circle your choice and explain your opinion.

1. Tom sees the money-making possibilities in nearly every situation.

right   **wrong**

_____
_____
_____

2. Mamma puts all the brothers together even though only one is sick.

right   **wrong**

_____
_____

3. John gives Tom his special Indian belt to end the silent treatment.

right   **wrong**

_____
_____
_____

4. Mr. Standish paddles and ruler slaps his misbehaving students.

right   **wrong**

_____
_____
_____

5. John helps Andy with his suicide attempts.

right   **wrong**

_____
_____

What I Liked — What I Learned

Work in small groups. Assign a character from this list to each group member. Each person writes what he or she has liked about and learned from the assigned character. After the ideas have been shared in the group, present them to the class.

Abie	John	Tom
Mamma	Andy	Papa

My Name _____

My Character _____

What I liked about _____ was

_____

_____

_____

_____

_____

_____

What I learned from _____ was

_____

_____

_____

_____

_____

_____

Owl Moon

by Jane Yolen

For a long time, a child has waited to go owling with Pa. And late one winter night, the time comes. Trudging out into the bright moonlit night, they begin their search for the Great Horned Owl.

Filled with anticipation and excitement, the child tries to keep up with Pa, remembering to be quiet. Pa calls the owl and they wait in breathless silence for an answer — close to nature, close to each other.

The call is answered and they spot the owl. What the child learns in the moments of watching and waiting is a lesson in hope that will stay with the child — and the reader — for a long, long time.

Setting

Create a picture of where and when the story took place.

The Purpose

Draw a box around the things from this list that happen in the story.

1. The family is tired from working all day in the fields.

2. The story takes place at night.

3. The child in the story has wanted to go owling for a long time.

4. To go owling, everyone needs a gun.

5. The older brothers have all been owling before.

6. The child goes owling with the mother.

7. It rains for most of the night.

8. Silence is important, and they are very quiet.

9. They see an owl.

10. The owl is brought home for a pet.

Do You Understand?

1.   Why did the child in the story go owling?

_____

_____

_____

2.   Did he or she really want to go? _____
Explain. _____

3.   Did Pa and the child expect to see an owl?_____
Explain. _____

_____

_____

_____

4.   What was the importance of silence during the owling adventure?

_____

_____

_____

5.   How did the child feel when the night's owling was over?

Hope

Read these quotes from the story. Write your ideas of what it means on the lines below.

1. "If you go owling you have to be quiet, . . . "

_____

_____

_____

_____

_____

_____

2. "When you go owling you have to be brave."

_____

_____

_____

_____

_____

_____

_____

3. "When you go owling you don't need words or warmth or anything but hope. That's what Pa says. The kind of hope that flies on silent wings under a shining Owl Moon."

_____

_____

_____

_____

_____

_____

_____

Use Your Senses

A good writer can make you feel what the characters in the story feel. Jane Yolen is just such a writer.

Write words and phrases from the story that make you see, hear, smell, taste, or touch what the characters in the story do.

APPLICATION: Activity 2

I've Been Waiting, Too.

The child in the story had been waiting a long time to go owling. This night was very special.

1. Is there something in your life you had to wait a long time for? _____
    What was it? _____
    _____
    _____
    _____
    _____
    _____

2. Why was it important to you? _____
    _____
    _____
    _____
    _____

3. How long did you have to wait for it? _____
    Was it worth waiting for? _____
    Explain. _____
    _____
    _____
    _____
    _____

Real Life?

Do you think a story like this one could happen in real life? _____

Explain your answer.

_____

_____

_____

Give three examples from the story that support your opinion.

1. _____

_____

_____

_____

2. _____

_____

_____

_____

_____

3. _____

_____

_____

_____

Could "going owling" ever happen in **your** life? _____

Explain your answer.

_____

_____

_____

_____

_____

The Power of Words

Jane Yolen uses words in such a way that we can sense what the characters in the story sense. One way she does this is by her use of *similies*. A *simile* compares two things using *like* or *as*.

Here are some similies from the story. Decide what is being compared. Then, explain what idea the comparison helps to communicate.

1. "The trees stood still as giant statues."

   Trees are compared to _____

   This comparison helps communicate the idea that _____

   _____

   _____

   _____

   _____

   _____

2. "And when their voices faded away, it was as quiet as a dream."

   The quiet in the woods is compared to the quiet in a _____

   This comparison helps communicate the idea that _____

   _____

   _____

   _____

   _____

3. "Then the owl pumped its great wings and lifted off the branch like a shadow without sound."

   The owl's lift off is compared to a _____

   This comparison helps communicate the idea that _____

   _____

   _____

   _____

   _____

The Power of Words

There are other comparisons in the story. Sometimes these comparisons use *like* or *as* and sometimes they do not.

Here is a list of incomplete comparisons from the book. Find the description that completes each comparison and write it in.

1. "Somewhere behind us a train whistle blew, long and low, like a _____

    _____

    _____

    _____

    _____."

2. "I could feel the cold as if someone's _____

    _____

    _____

    _____

    _____."

3. "My _____ felt _____, for the scarf over it was wet and warm."

4. "It seemed to fit exactly over the center of the clearing and the snow below it was whiter than _____

    _____

    _____

    _____."

5. "But I was a _____

    _____

    _____

    _____

    as we walked home."

Talk about what you think each of these comparisons means.

Whoo-whoo-who-who-who-whooo!

Have a class owl calling contest! Practice for this event by listening to recordings of owls and repeating those sounds. Also practice the call which is the title of this page. Then, let the contest begin!

Write the name of each owl caller on this chart. Give each person a score of 1 to 5, with 5 being the best. The owl caller who has the most points or attracts a **real** owl wins!

name	score	name	score

The Owl and Us

The way the owl answers Pa's call makes the child think the two of them are talking about supper, or the woods, or the moon, or the cold.

Work in groups of three. Pretend you are Pa, the owl, and the child. Write what you suppose might be a conversation the three of them could have. Perform your dialogue for the class!

_____   _____

                       _____

                       _____

_____   _____

                       _____

                       _____

_____   _____

                       _____

                       _____

_____   _____

                       _____

                       _____

_____   _____

                       _____

                       _____

_____   _____

                       _____

                       _____

_____   _____

                       _____

                       _____

_____   _____

Owling

1. What can be learned from owling? _____
    _____
    _____
    _____

2. Is it important to learn these things?_____
    Explain your answer. _____
    _____
    _____
    _____

3. Would you like to go owling? _____
    Why? _____
    _____
    _____

4. Who would you go with? _____
    Why? _____
    _____
    _____

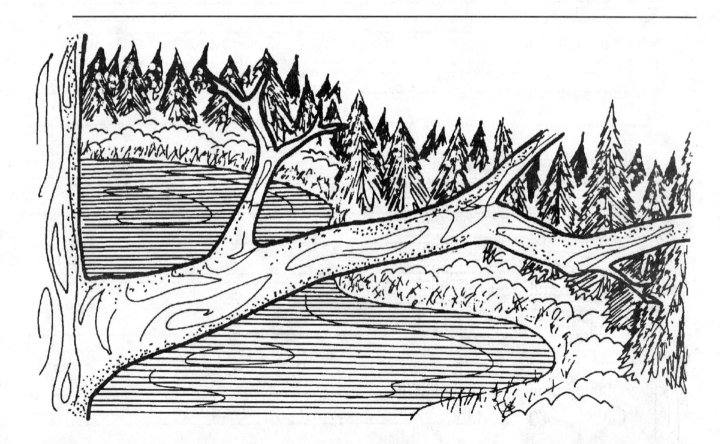

62

Owling and Pa

The child in the story looked forward to the day he or she could go owling with Pa.

1. Why do you think going owling was so important to the child? _____

_____

_____

_____

_____

_____

2. Do you think that being alone with Pa was just as important? _____
Explain. _____

_____

_____

_____

_____

3. What do you think means more to the child: Owling or alone time with Pa? _____

Explain your choice. _____

_____

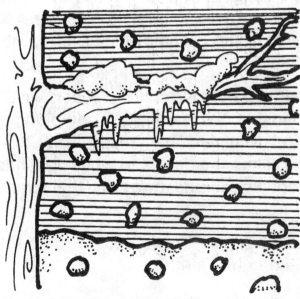

_____

_____

_____

_____

_____

_____

_____

_____

_____

On My Honor

by Marion Dane Bauer

Tony and Joel are best friends and, like best friends, do nearly everything together. Tony is the daring one, and often suggests that they adventure in reckless ways. And the day the story takes place proves to be no exception. He cons the more cautious Joel into a long bike ride to the Starved Rock Bluffs, with a dangerous rock climb as the goal.

On the way, Tony is sidetracked by the swiftly-moving Vermillion River, which sparks his interest in a dangerous swim. Against Joel's warnings, Tony plunges in, daring Joel to follow. Joel does, and finds himself challenging Tony to a sandbar swim. Although not a swimmer, Tony takes the dare and while Joel has his eyes on the sandbar destination, is swept under and away by the strong currents.

What follows is Joel's attempt to deal with his friend Tony's death — and the anger, guilt, and emptiness that overwhelm him in his grief.

pages 64 - 79

p. 96

1 Copy each

Who Said That?

Match the characters with what they said.

Mr. Bates   Bobby

Joel   Mrs. Zabrinsky

teenage boy   Tony

---

1. _____ "He tried swimming lessons once, but he was always afraid of the water."

2. _____ "I believe there's something about life that goes on. It seems too good to end in a river."

3. _____ "Look...do you know...how long...it takes...somebody...to drown?"

4. _____ "Well, are you coming in, or are you just going to stand there and gawk?"

5. _____ "Joel's gonna let me help him with his paper route tomorrow, too."

6. _____ "I tried to stop him. I told him the river was dangerous."

The River

Draw the Vermillion River and what Tony leaves behind on its bank.

Chapter 4

You have just finished reading Chapter 3. It has ended with Joel saying, "We'll see who's chicken." What do you think will happen next? Write your ideas for Chapter 4.

Chapter 4

_____

_____

_____

_____

_____

_____

_____

_____

_____

_____

_____

_____

_____

_____

_____

Quotes

Explain what these quotes mean in the story.

1. "But he didn't know what kept him and Tony together except that, after Tony, other kids seemed boring." (Chapter 1)

    _____

    _____

    _____

    _____

    _____

    _____

    _____

2. "It was all Tony's fault. All of it! Tony knew what a poor swimmer he was. He had to have realized the risks. And now he had gone off and left Joel to answer for him. And what was he going to say?" (Chapter 9)

    _____

    _____

    _____

    _____

    _____

    _____

    _____

3. "Joel lifted his arm to his nose and sniffed. The smell was still there, so sharp that it made his eyes sting. He supposed it would be with him the rest of his life." (Chapter 12)

    _____

    _____

    _____

    _____

    _____

    _____

    _____

What If...?

How would the story have changed if...

1.　...Joel's father had not given permission for the long ride?

_____

_____

_____

_____

2.　...there were people having a picnic by Tony's Vermillion River spot?

_____

_____

_____

3.　...Joel had refused to go in the river with Tony?

_____

_____

_____

_____

4.　...Joel had gone to the police with the teenage boy to inform them of Tony's drowning?

_____

_____

_____

5.　...Joel never told anyone the truth about Tony?

_____

_____

_____

Tell Us, Tony.

We know what Tony does in the story, but we do not know what he thinks.
Pretend you are Tony and answer these questions.

1. What is your favorite...
    color? _____
    food? _____
    book? _____
    T.V. show?_____
    place to go? _____
    subject in school? _____

2. Why is Joel your best friend?

    _____
    _____
    _____
    _____

3. What makes you do dangerous things?

    _____
    _____
    _____
    _____

4. How did you feel when Joel dared you to swim to the sandbar?

    _____
    _____
    _____

5. Why did you try to swim to the sandbar?

    _____
    _____
    _____

6. Would you do it again if you had it to do over again? _____
    Explain. _____

    _____
    _____
    _____

What Is The Truth?

Write "TRUE" next to each sentence that is true in the story. Write "FALSE" next to each sentence that is not true. Be ready to explain the reasons for your "FALSE" answers.

1. _____ Tony is a reckless boy only around Joel.

2. _____ Joel would love to have Tony as a brother.

3. _____ Tony has permission to ride to Starved Rock.

4. _____ Joel and Tony go to Starved Rock before they swim in the Vermillion River.

5. _____ The junior high swim team coach trains swimmers in the Vermillion River.

6. _____ While they are playing in the river, Joel and Tony joke about the possibility of Tony drowning.

7. _____ No one actually sees Tony drown.

8. _____ Joel immediately tells the police about Tony.

9. _____ Joel blames himself for Tony's accident.

10. _____ Joel's father punishes Joel severely for the lies he tells.

Joel and Tony

Joel and Tony are friends. They are both 12 years old, and that's where the similarity ends. Write some of their differences here.

JOEL BATES	**TONY ZABRINSKY**
_____	_____
_____	_____
_____	_____
_____	_____
_____	_____
_____	_____
_____	_____
_____	_____
_____	_____
_____	_____

Which person are you more like?_____

Explain. _____

_____

_____

_____

72

DANGER!

Work with a partner. Make a list of places in the area where you live that are or could be dangerous for children. Next to each place, explain why it is dangerous.

AREA	DANGER

DANGER!

Work with your partner to create warning signs for each dangerous area you listed on page 1 of this activity.

WARNING

I DARE YOU!

Work with your class to make a list of ten dares.

1. _____

2. _____

3. _____

4. _____

5. _____

6. _____

7. _____

8. _____

9. _____

10. _____

I DARE YOU!

Prepare for a class debate concerning the dares you listed on page 1 of this activity. Write reasons to take or not to take each dare. Then have a class debate to present your ideas.

Reasons To Take Dare	Reasons Not To Take Dare
1. _____	1. _____
2. _____	2. _____
3. _____	3. _____
4. _____	4. _____
5. _____	5. _____
6. _____	6. _____
7. _____	7. _____
8. _____	8. _____
9. _____	9. _____
10. _____	10. _____

BE THE JUDGE!

Judge the actions of these characters in the story.

1. Joel did not want to go bike riding to Starved Rock. However, he went.

   _____

   _____

   _____

   _____

   _____

2. Tony could not swim. He decided to go "swimming" in the Vermillion River.

   _____

   _____

   _____

   _____

3. Joel noticed Tony thrashing instead of swimming in the water. He challenged Tony to the sandbar swim contest anyway.

   _____

   _____

   _____

   _____

4. Joel knew what happened to Tony. He lied to his parents and Tony's parents.

   _____

   _____

   _____

   _____

WHICH OF THESE THINGS MIGHT YOU HAVE DONE?

Circle your answer.

| #1 | #2 | #3 | #4 | None of them |

FRIENDSHIP

What brings friends together?

_____

_____

Read this list of things that might bring friends together. Write each thing on the list below in the order of its importance to **you** (#1 is most important).

neighborhood	age
sports	hobbies
parents	pets
books	school
scouts	toys

1. _____

2. _____

3. _____

4. _____

5. _____

6. _____

7. _____

8. _____

9. _____

10. _____

What things on the list brought Joel and Tony together? _____

_____

FRIENDSHIP

What keeps friends together?

_____

_____

Read this list of qualities that friends might look for in each other. Write each quality on the list below in the order of its importance to **you** (#1 is most important).

funny	brave
athletic	creative
quiet	loyal
understanding	reckless
smart	loving
attractive	honest

1. _____
2. _____
3. _____
4. _____
5. _____
6. _____
7. _____
8. _____
9. _____
10. _____
11. _____
12. _____

What qualities on the list do you think were important to Joel and Tony's friendship? _____

The Reluctant Dragon

by Kenneth Grahame

In the English countryside long ago, a dragon is sighted by a shepherd. His young son, well-versed in dragon lore, agrees to talk with the beast. Through their conversation, the boy learns that the dragon is not the usual snorting, fire-breathing, wreaking-havoc sort of a dragon. On the contrary, this dragon is a gentle poet who abhors violence, and is a bit on the lazy side.

However, the prejudiced townspeople assume without cause that the intruder in their countryside is quite dangerous. They anxiously await for the arrival of their hero, St. George, to vanquish the enemy. Upon his arrival, the boy convinces St. George to meet with the dragon before engaging in battle.

The meeting begins their friendship, and a plan emerges that will make all winners - the boy, the dragon, St. George, and the fight-provoking townspeople.

WANTED!

Three characters have escaped from Kenneth Grahame's story, *The Reluctant Dragon*. Please help in their "capture" by supplying all the information you can.

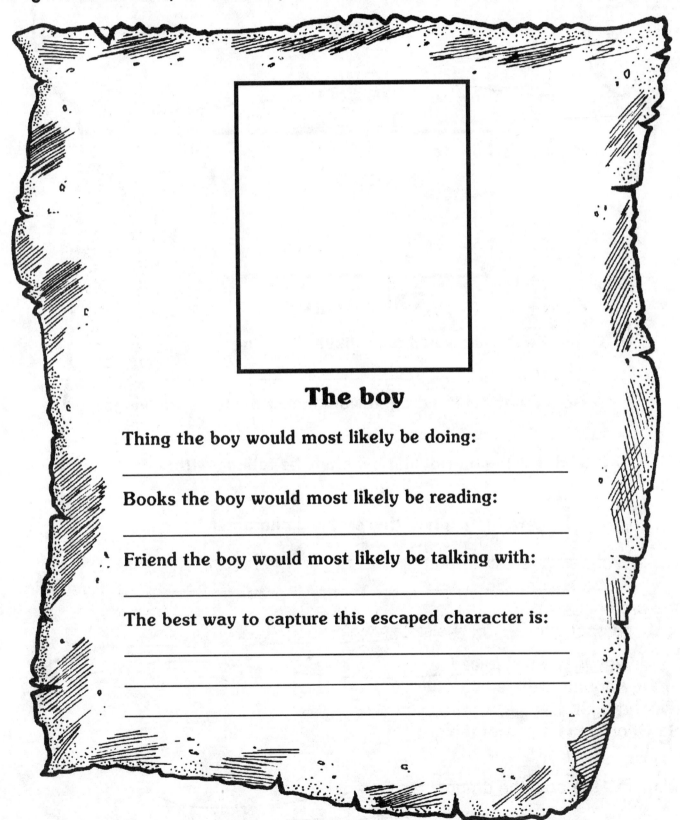

The boy

Thing the boy would most likely be doing:

_____

Books the boy would most likely be reading:

_____

Friend the boy would most likely be talking with:

_____

The best way to capture this escaped character is:

_____

_____

_____

WANTED!

The dragon

Thing the dragon would most likely be doing:

_____

Personality traits the dragon would most likely be showing:

_____

Friend the dragon would most likely be talking with:

_____

The best way to capture this escaped character is:

_____

_____

WANTED!

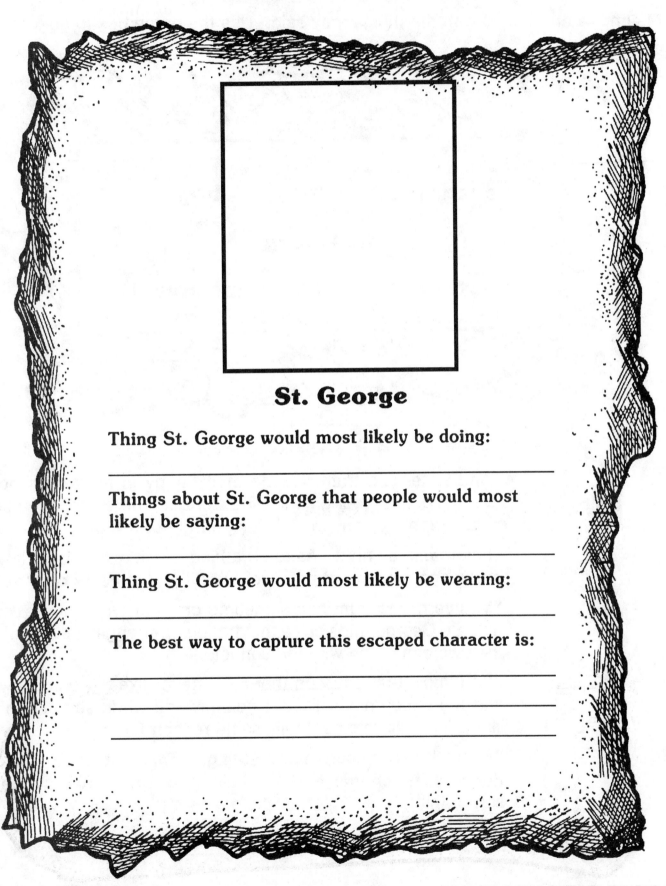

St. George

Thing St. George would most likely be doing:

_____

Things about St. George that people would most likely be saying:

_____

Thing St. George would most likely be wearing:

_____

The best way to capture this escaped character is:

_____

_____

_____

Who Said That?

Match the characters with the things they said. Use the name box to help you.

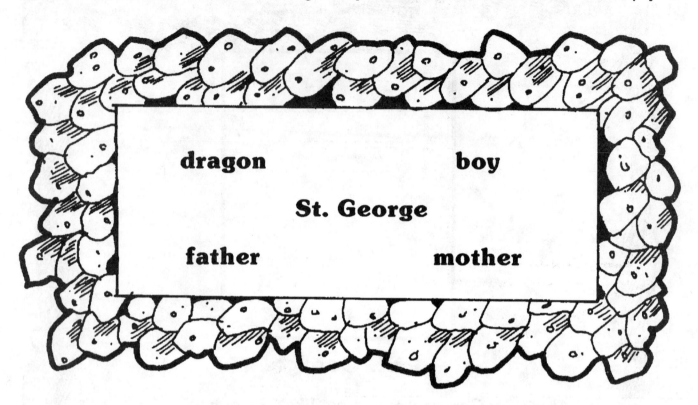

dragon   boy

St. George

father   mother

1. _____ "And to tell the truth, I'm not half happy in my own mind, thinking of that poor animal lying alone up there, without a bit o' hot supper or anyone to change the news with..."

2. _____ "I can *ramp* all right. As to breathing fire, it's surprising how easily one gets out of practice; but I'll do the best I can."

3. _____ "You've *got* to fight him sometime or other, you know, 'cos he's St. George and you're the dragon. Better get it over, and then we can go on with the sonnets."

4. _____ "You know that cave up there — I never liked it, somehow, and the sheep never liked it neither, and when sheep don't like a thing there's generally some reason for it."

5. _____ "*Knew* I had forgotten something. There ought to be a Princess, terror-stricken and chained to a rock, and all that sort of thing."

84

Our Reasons

What are the reasons the three characters below have for organizing and carrying out the combat on the Downs? Draw their pictures on the shields.

The boy:

_____

_____

_____

_____

St. George:

_____

_____

_____

_____

_____

The dragon:

_____

_____

_____

_____

COMPREHENSION: Activity 2

What Do They Mean?

Explain what the following quotes mean in the story.

1. "Oh, yes, a peaceable sort o' beast enough, and not ramping or carrying on or doing anything but what was quite right and proper. I admit all that. And yet, what am I to do? Scales, you know, and claws, and a tail for certain, though I didn't see that end of him — I ain't used to 'em, and I don't hold with 'em, and that's a fact!"

_____

_____

_____

_____

2. "This is an evil world, and sometimes I begin to think that all the wickedness in it is not entirely bottled up inside the dragons."

_____

_____

_____

_____

3. "But the whole thing's nonsense, and conventionality, and popular thick-headedness. There's absolutely nothing to fight about, from beginning to end."

_____

_____

_____

DRAGON ENCOUNTER!

You have changed places with the boy and the dragon. It is your first meeting. Work with a partner to create the dialogue. When finished, share your conversation with the class!

_____

_____

_____

_____

_____

_____

_____

_____

_____

_____

_____

_____

_____

_____

_____

_____

_____

_____

_____

_____

_____

_____

Now Serving!

The dragon in the story doesn't appear to be a hunter. We don't see him gathering carrots near his home either. What does this dragon eat?

Plan out a dinner you think he will enjoy. Also include how it will be served as well as how he will be entertained while dining.

Your dinner menu will be

_____
_____
_____
_____
_____
_____
_____
_____
_____
_____
_____
_____

The meal will be served

_____
_____
_____
_____
_____

Your entertainment will be

_____
_____
_____
_____
_____
_____

88

Dragon Differences

The reluctant dragon is not a typical dragon. How is he different from the typical fairy tale dragons?

The Reluctant Dragon

_____

_____

_____

_____

_____

_____

_____

The Fairy Tale Dragon

_____

_____

_____

_____

_____

_____

_____

_____

_____

_____

FACT or FAIRY TALE?

Decide which of the things below could happen in real life and which could only happen in a fairy tale. Circle your choice.

1. **Fact** | **Fairy Tale** — A boy enjoys reading books about history and fairy tales.

2. **Fact** | **Fairy Tale** — A dragon purrs happily and thinks poetic thoughts.

3. **Fact** | **Fairy Tale** — A boy and a dragon have a conversation.

4. **Fact** | **Fairy Tale** — The people of a town love to watch a good fight.

5. **Fact** | **Fairy Tale** — A dragon killer works out a deal with a dragon — a deal in which they *both* "win."

6. **Fact** | **Fairy Tale** — A hero tells the people of a town not to be so fond of fighting, not to be prejudiced, and not to make up wild stories.

7. **Fact** | **Fairy Tale** — A dragon becomes the star of a party, loved and accepted by the townspeople.

Dragon Verse

The reluctant dragon is not reluctant when it comes to creating poetry!
Write a poem that you think the dragon could have written himself.

DRAGON Contest!

Create your own dragon using any materials that are appropriate, (paper, yarn, foil, dried beans, clips, buttons, sandpaper, "jewels," pasta, etc.). Make it as large as your teacher allows. Attach this dragon information sheet to your dragon on a class bulletin board display. Choose the most creative, scariest, funniest, silliest, or any other "most" your class would like!

My DRAGON!

Name: _____

Age: _____ Height: _____ Weight: _____

Colors: _____

Favorite thing to do: _____

_____

_____

Favorite place to be: _____

_____

_____

Favorite food: _____

Favorite thing to say: _____

_____

Friends: _____

_____

Enemies: _____

_____

This dragon was created by: _____

Were They Right?

Were these three characters right to carry out the fight?

I think the boy _____ have promoted the fight because _____
  (should/should not)

_____

_____

_____

_____

_____

_____

I think St. George _____ have fought with the dragon because
  (should/should not)

_____

_____

_____

_____

_____

_____

_____

I think the dragon _____ have fought with St. George because
  (should/should not)

_____

_____

_____

_____

_____

_____

_____

More Than A Fairy Tale...

This story is more than a fairy tale. It can teach us about values that may be important in our lives.

1. Can learning to not be so fond of fighting help you in your life? _____
   Explain. _____
   _____
   _____
   _____
   _____

2. Can learning to tell the truth instead of making up colorful, somewhat believable stories to replace the truth help you in your life? _____
   Explain. _____
   _____
   _____
   _____
   _____

3. Can learning that all dragons are not the same and should not be treated as if they are, help in your life? _____
   Explain. _____
   _____
   _____
   _____
   _____

ANSWER KEY

The Hundred Dresses

K-1 The girls saw an empty square room, with absolutely nothing left in it. An empty closet was visible in the corner also.

K-2
1.	Miss Mason	2.	Maddie
3.	Wanda	4.	Peggy
5.	Maddie	6.	Jake
7.	Wanda	8.	Jan Petronski
9.	Peggy	10.	Maddie

C-1 Dress pictures should be drawn.
1. Miss Mason had covered the walls and bulletin board in her classroom with Wanda's 100 dresses, to show very graphically why Wanda had won the contest, etc.
2. When people saw Wanda's artwork, they were overwhelmed with the beauty of her designs and clapped. Peggy and Maddie felt terrible because of the teasing they had done. Wanda really did have 100 dresses, etc.
3. They could do nothing because Wanda had moved — Peggy and Maddie tried to make contact, etc.

C-2
1. Maddie is afraid that she may become the center of the joking, because she is also poor. She would be crushed by the cruelty the girls have shown Wanda, etc.
2. Peggy "lives" to tease Wanda, for her own enjoyment and to the delight of the friends around her, etc.
3. Mr. Petronski is being forced to leave the town because of the prejudicial behavior directed towards his children, etc.
4. Maddie shows her growth and compassion for others as she resolves never to stand silently by when she knows something is wrong, etc.

An-1 Peggy: rich; self-centered; cruel without any knowledge of her cruelty; long, curly auburn hair; great dresser; first to tease, etc.

Maddie: poor; thinks about others; sensitive; short, straight blond hair; wears hand-me-downs; courageous, etc.

An-2
1.	Peggy	2.	Wanda
3.	Wanda	4.	Maddie
5.	Peggy	6.	Wanda
7.	Maddie	8.	Wanda
9.	Peggy	10.	Maddie

The Cay

K-1
1.	2	2.	4
3.	1	4.	6
5.	5	6.	8
7.	3	8.	9
9.	7	10.	10

K-2 Age: More than 70 (first says over 60, then amends it)
Description: Old, black man; muscular, huge, wiry gray-white hair, welt on left cheek, etc.
Favorite words: "Dat be true", "Outrageous", etc.
Personality description: Kind, giving, willing to teach Phillip at his own rate, wise, clear-thinking, unselfish, genuine, humorous, etc.
Special friends: Phillip and, on occasion, Stew Cat

C-1 Phillip should be drawn tied to the palm tree, protected by Timothy's tied body.
1. The hurricane that "destroys" the cay is pictured.

2. The cay is devastated by the hurricane, Timothy dies, Phillip "rebuilds" his island home, Phillip is rescued, etc.
3. Timothy makes thorough preparations — high ground, rope tied on palm, water keg secured, etc.
4. Timothy protects Phillip with his life. Phillip respects Timothy's wisdom, etc.

C-2
1. Phillip believes Blacks are inferior, etc.
2. Phillip wants Timothy's friendship — Timothy says he already has it, etc.
3. Phillip is beginning to realize that color has nothing to do with warmth and comfort, etc.
4. Phillip does not "see" color lines drawn between people. Timothy is Timothy, and Phillip loves him, etc.

An-1 Check for appropriate responses.

An-2
1.	False	2.	False
3.	True	4.	True
5.	False	6.	False
7.	True	8.	True
9.	True	10.	False
11.	False	12.	True

The Great Brain

K-1
1.	e	2.	f
3.	h	4.	i
5.	c	6.	j
7.	g	8.	b
9.	d	10.	a

K-2
1. Tom's mother makes them refund the money to all the children because they have been promised a free viewing. And 20 children get in line for refunds a second time, so Tom actually loses 20 cents!
2. S.D. and T.D. get so angry with J.D. they give him the silent treatment. J.D. can't stand for his brothers to be silent toward him so he trades his special Indian belt to break the silence.
3. The alcoholic frame works, but Mr. Standish's reputation is on the line and Tom's father makes him confess his master plan. Tom does come out a winner, even though the plan to fire the teacher backfires. Mr. Standish is proud of Tom's courage to confess and decides to change his harsh punishment rules, making Tom a hero to his classmates.

C-1 Tom comes to the realization that what he does for Andy is its own reward and that Andy should keep the erector set. Seeing Andy "whole" again makes Tom happier than owning the erector set would. This is a "first" for money-minded Tom.

C-2
1. Mr. Leeds is an intolerant man who hates immigrants. He cannot see beyond his prejudice and has taught Sammy to be the same way. Papa explains the beauty of differences to his son Tom, something Mr. Leeds does not do for Sammy, which is why Sammy picks on Basil.
2. Abie's empty strongbox does not hold gold. Had he let the town know that, he would have had to live on charity — something his pride would not let him do.
3. Tom is touched by the warm feeling he has when he tells Andy to keep the erector set. Tom decides to give the Indian belt that he had "confiscated" back to his brother, also.

Owl Moon

K-1 The picture should be of a snow-covered woods, late at night with a bright, clearly visible moon. No wind is blowing the trees in the woods.

K-2   Numbers 2, 3, 5, 8, and 9 should be boxed.

C-1
1. The child went owling because it was a "coming of age" experience that had been long awaited with eagerness, etc.
2. Yes, owling was a grand adventure, up to now kept only for his or her brothers and Pa, etc.
3. No, the brothers had warned that sometimes you see an owl, sometimes you don't, etc.
4. All the forest noises must be heard clearly, so human noise was unwanted, etc.
5. The child was thoroughly touched by the experience, to the point that he or she remained in silence on the trip home. Owling was all the child had hoped it would be, a chance to learn from silence, to appreciate nature, and become closer to Pa, etc.

C-2
1. If you want to see an owl, silence is essential, otherwise the owl will possibly be frightened away by your noise, etc.
2. When you go owling, you can't be frightened of noises from things you can't see or things you imagine might be there, etc.
3. The hope that an owl will be spotted is all that is needed to go owling. Warmth and words are not needed, Pa says. It is the hope that is fulfilled in the heart of a child by seeing an owl on silent wings fly on a bright moonlit night, and becoming closer to nature, etc.

An-1   This story could happen in real life. Examples are throughout the text.

An-2   (page 1)
1. Giant statues: Statues are stone still, as were the trees that night, etc.
2. Dream: Dreams are ethereal and quiet — also, it must be in a quiet sleep state that one has a dream, etc.
3. Shadow without sound: Shadows make no noise — neither did the owl when it took flight, etc.

An-2   (page 2)
1. sad, sad song
2. icy hand was palm-down on my back
3. mouth/furry
4. the milk in a cereal bowl
5. shadow

On Your Honor

K-1
1. Mrs. Zabrinsky
2. Mr. Bates
3. teenage boy
4. Tony
5. Bobby
6. Joel

K-2   Description of the Vermillion River: Large, swift, oily-looking, reddish, muddy, current/whirlpool dangers, etc.

What was left on the bank: Tony's bike (old, red paint-flecked, no fenders or handlegrips); his faded blue t-shirt; jeans; underwear; sneakers

C-2
1. Even though Joel did not have "much in common" with Tony, Joel felt that Tony was exciting and Joel never had a dull moment with him, etc.
2. Tony's recklessness was the cause of his death, because he knew his lack of swimming ability could be fatal. And he was not there to help Joel tell about the reckless drowning. Joel was at a loss about what to say.
3. Joel thought the smell of the river would remain on his body as a perpetual reminder of Tony's death, and the part Joel played in that death, etc.

An-1
1. FALSE - Tony was often reckless, with or without Joel, e.g. the hang gliding with a sheet incident.
2. TRUE
3. FALSE - He did not ask his mother.

4. FALSE - They never make it to Starved Rock.
5. FALSE - The river training was Tony's idea, not the coach's.
6. TRUE
7. TRUE
8. FALSE - He didn't want to tell the police — even fabricating a lie to keep from doing so. Joel finally did, but not willingly.
9. TRUE
10. FALSE - Mr. Bates was compassionate, accepting the blame for Tony's death and sharing greatly in Joel's loss.

An-2   Joel - conservative; responsible; inclined to be cautious; worries about Tony's recklessness; one younger brother; great new bike; smaller and lighter than Tony; strong swimmer; etc.

Tony - daring; not exceptionally responsible; reckless; "worries" about Joel's over-cautiousness; takes wild dares; bigger and heavier than Joel; non-swimmer; hand-me-down bike; large family; etc.

The Reluctant Dragon

K-1   Answers will vary on each of these posters, but here are some general ideas.

The boy - most likely be reading or talking with the dragon; most likely be reading book about natural history and fairy tales; most likely be talking with the dragon; could be captured by the lure of a good book or a dragon in the vicinity, etc.

The dragon - most likely be relaxing and composing poetry; most likely be contemplative, poetical, mellow, pleasant, etc.; most likely be talking with the boy; could be captured by the lure of poetry reading, someone interested in his poetry, or a fine banquet, etc.

St. George - most likely be righting wrongs, people would most likely be saying what a wonderful brave man he is; most likely be wearing fluted armor inlaid with gold and a plumed helmet; could be captured by the lure of injustice, etc.

K-2
1. mother
2. dragon
3. boy
4. father
5. St. George

C-1   Answers will vary, but here are some general ideas.
1. The boy wants the fight to happen because it must happen, the townspeople won't rest until it does. Then, after the fight, the dragon and the boy can continue their friendship, uninterrupted by prejudice and fear, etc.
2. The dragon sees the fight as his "ticket" to acceptance in society, where he can reveal his endearing qualities, etc.
3. St. George regards the fight as his duty. He is called upon by the townspeople in a business sense, and being a heroic type, will not shirk his responsibility, etc.

C-2
1. Even though the father sees the dragon as peaceable, his past prejudice about dragons enters in, making it difficult for him to see one dragon as different from any other dragon, etc.
2. St. George begins to think that there are other sources of wrongdoing, aside from dragons, etc.
3. The dragon believes the impending fight to be ridiculous, based only on the tradition of dragon fighting, and the people who are a party to it are rather stupid. He sees no cause for fighting, etc.

An-1   The reluctant dragon is meditative, peaceable, right and proper, non-violent, poetical, lazy, social, kind, etc. A stereotype dragon is a fighter and murderer, breathes fire and bellows smoke, is a scourge on society, etc.

An-2   FACT   1, 4, 6

FAIRY TALE   2, 3, 5, 7